JAN 2 2 2007

11/13

ELK GROVE VILLAGE PUBLIC LIBRARY

3 1250 00765 9307

W9-BAC-421

Discarded By Elk Grove
Village Public Library

ELK GROVE VILLAGE PUBLIC LIBRARY
1001 WELLINGTON AVE
ELK GROVE VILLAGE, IL 60007
(847) 439-0447

SAVE OUR ANIMALS!

Asian Elephant

Louise and Richard Spilsbury

Heinemann Library
Chicago, Illinois

© 2006 Heinemann Library
a division of Reed Elsevier Inc.
Chicago, Illinois

Customer Service 888–454–2279

Visit our website at www.heinemannlibrary.com

All rights reserved. No part of this publication may be reproduced or transmitted in any form
or by any means, electronic or mechanical, including photocopying, recording, taping, or any
information storage and retrieval system, without permission in writing from the publisher.

Photo research by Hannah Taylor and Fiona Orbell
Designed by Michelle Lisseter and Ron Kamen
Printed in China, by South China Printing Co. Ltd.

10 09 08 07 06
10 9 8 7 6 5 4 3 2 1

Library of Congress Cataloging-in-Publication Data
Spilsbury, Louise.
Save the Asian elephant / Richard and Louise Spilsbury
      p. cm. – (Save our animals!)
Includes bibliographical references and index.
ISBN 1-4034-7802-3 (library binding-hardcover) -- ISBN 1-4034-7810-4 (pbk.)
    1. Asiatic elephant--Juvenile literature. 2. Asiatic
elephant--Conservation--Juvenile literature. I. Spilsbury, Richard,
1963- II. Title. III. Series.

QL737.P98S67 2006
599.67'6--dc22

                       2005027450

Acknowledgments
The author and publisher are grateful to the following for permission to reproduce copyright
material: Ardea pp. **4** top (Y A Betrand), **5** top left, **13, 26–27, 29** (J Rajput), **22**; Steve Bloom p. **28**;
Corbis p. **25** (M Harvey); Digital Vision p. **5** middle; Ecoscene p. **10** (W Lawler); FLPA p. **15**
(J Zimmerman); Naturepl.com p. **4** bottom left (M Carwardine); NHPA pp. **12** (N Garbutt), **23**
(A & S Toon); Oxford Scientific pp. **4** middle, **5** top right, **6, 7** (S Camazine), **9** (M Brooke), **11**
(Animals Animals), **14** (D Murrell), **16** (M Sewell), **18** (A Desai), **21, 24**; Panos Pictures p. **19**
(A Vitale); Still Pictures pp. **5** bottom; **17** (J Kaplan).

Cover photograph of Asian elephant, reproduced with permission of NHPA/Andy Rouse.

The publishers would like to thank Sarala Khaling at WWF in Nepal for her assistance in the
preparation of this book.

Every effort has been made to contact copyright holders of any material reproduced in this
book. Any omissions will be rectified in subsequent printings if notice is given to the publisher.

Disclaimer
All Internet addresses (URLs) given in this book were valid at the time of going to press.
However, due to the dynamic nature of the Internet, some addresses may have changed or
ceased to exist since publication. While the author and the publishers regret any inconvenience
this may cause readers, no responsibility for any such changes can be accepted by either the
author or the publishers.

Some words are shown in bold, **like this**. You can find out what they mean
by looking in the glossary.

Contents

Animals in Trouble

There are many different types, or **species**, of animals. Some species are in danger of becoming **extinct**. This means that all the animals from that species might die.

All the animals shown here are in danger of becoming extinct. These species need to be saved. The Asian elephant is one of them.

The Asian Elephant

Elephants have huge gray bodies and big ears. They use their long trunks for smelling, touching, and holding things.

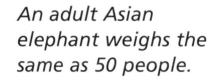

An adult Asian elephant weighs the same as 50 people.

Some **male** Asian elephants have two long teeth called **tusks**.

There are African elephants and Asian elephants. The Asian elephant has a shorter trunk and smaller ears than the African elephant.

Where Can You Find Asian Elephants?

Asian elephants live in thirteen of the countries on the **continent** of **Asia**. Over half of all Asian elephants live in India.

Wild Asian elephants live where there are not many people.

BHUTAN
CHINA
NEPAL
A S I A
INDIA
MYANMAR (BURMA)
LAOS
THAILAND
BANGLADESH
VIETNAM
CAMBODIA
SRI LANKA
MALAYSIA
Equator
Borneo
Sumatra
INDONESIA

N
W
E
S

0   400   800 Miles
0   400   800 Kilometers

Asian elephants drink water from lakes or rivers.

Asian elephants live in forests where there are patches of long grass between the trees. It is usually hot and dry there. This is the Asian elephant's **habitat**.

What Do Asian Elephants Eat?

Elephants are **herbivores**, which means they only eat plants. Elephants eat grass, leaves, and **roots**. They also eat **bark** and fruit from trees.

Elephants spend most of the day eating.

Every day, Asian elephants eat the same weight of food as 600 loaves of bread!

Elephants sometimes use their trunks to reach leaves at the top of trees. Then they put the leaves into their mouths with their trunks.

Young Asian Elephants

A baby elephant is called a calf. An elephant calf can stand up soon after it is born. After two or three days, it can follow its mother around.

Elephants are **mammals**, so the babies drink their mothers' milk.

Adult elephants protect the calves from attack.

Asian elephants live in a group called a herd. The babies grow up and play together. The adults in the herd look after the young elephants.

Working Elephants

It is against the law to catch wild elephants, but some people still do. They make the elephants carry big logs. The elephants sometimes die from working too hard.

Elephants can carry logs where trucks cannot go.

Sometimes people make wild elephants work in a circus. Some get sick and die. Others die because they do not get the right food or enough room to exercise.

Some people feel it is wrong to keep elephants in a circus.

Hunting Asian Elephants

People used to kill **male** Asian elephants to get their **tusks**. Tusks are made of **ivory**. People carved the ivory or made piano keys from it.

Some ivory is used to make items like these.

If people buy tins of elephant meat, these animals may soon be **extinct**.

Some people hunt elephants for their skin and meat. The skin can be made into bags and boots. Sometimes people use it to make **traditional** medicines.

Dangers to the Asian Elephant's World

Asian elephants are losing their **habitat**. People are cutting down the forests where the elephants live. They use the wood to build towns there.

When forests are cut down, elephants have less space and less food.

Asian elephants can eat farmers' **crops** and damage people's homes. People sometimes kill the elephants to stop them.

People go hungry if elephants damage their crops.

How Many Asian Elephants Are There?

Around 100 years ago, there were more than 100,000 Asian elephants living in the wild. Today there are only about 35,000 wild Asian elephants.

100 years ago

Now

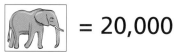 = 20,000

This graph shows how many Asian elephants there are.

The number of Asian elephants in the wild is still going down.

Adult Asian elephants are not in danger from other animals. They are too big and strong. They are in danger of becoming **extinct** because people do not look after them or their **habitat**.

How Are Asian Elephants Being Saved?

Some countries have areas of land where elephants are safe and their **habitat** is looked after. These areas are called **national parks**.

National parks are big because the elephants and other animals there need a lot of space.

These wardens stop poachers from killing elephants.

Poachers kill elephants for the **ivory** from their **tusks**. **Wardens** carry weapons because it is their job to stop the poachers.

Who Is Helping Asian Elephants?

Groups of people are working to save elephants. They raise money to pay for safe areas of land. They help train veterinarians who can help sick elephants.

This vet is helping an elephant that has a hurt foot.

WWF is a group that works to protect elephant **habitats.** It plants new trees. It also helps people understand why elephants need to be saved.

People need to learn how to protect elephants.

How Can You Help?

It is important to know that Asian elephants are in danger. Then you can learn how to help save them. Read, watch, and find out all you can about Asian elephants.

Here are some things you can do to help.

- Join a group that raises money for Asian elephants, such as **WWF**.
- Never buy **ivory** souvenirs.

The Future for Asian Elephants

There are very few wild elephants left in **Asia**. In the future, there may be none at all. There will only be working elephants or elephants in zoos.

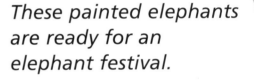

These painted elephants are ready for an elephant festival.

Let's hope that more Asian elephants will be safe in the future.

People should stop buying and selling **ivory**. We should protect elephants in **national parks**. Then the number of Asian elephants will grow again.

Asian Elephant Facts

- Asian elephants can live for about 60 years in the wild.
- An elephant's trunk can lift heavy logs, but it can also pick up things as small as a coin.
- Elephants are good swimmers. They can swim for several hours without a break.
- An elephant drinks by sucking the water up into its trunk and blowing it into its mouth.

Find Out More

Hodgson Meeker, Clare. *Hansa: The True Story of an Asian Elephant Baby*. Seattle: Sasquatch Books, 2002.

Spilsbury, Richard and Louise. *A Herd of Elephants*. Chicago: Heinemann Library, 2004.

Web Sites

To find out more about **WWF,** visit their Web site:

www.worldwildlife.org

Glossary

bark   hard layer that covers a tree trunk

continent   large area of land divided into different countries

crop   plant grown for food, such as bananas

extinct   when all the animals in a species die out and the species no longer exists

habitat   place where plants and animals grow and live

herbivore   animal that only eats plants

ivory   hard, white material that tusks are made of

male   animal that can become a father when it grows up. Men and boys are male people.

mammal   animal that feeds its babies with the mother's milk and has some hair on its body

national park   area of land where animals are protected and their habitat is looked after

poacher   someone who hunts animals when it is against the law to do so

root   part of a plant that grows underground

species   group of animals that can have babies together

traditional   something that has been done the same way for many years

tusk   long pointed front tooth of an elephant

warden   person who guards national parks

WWF   charity that helps endangered species. It is also called the World Wildlife Fund.

Index